point no point

Books by Jane Munro

Daughters (1982)
The Trees Just Moved into a Season of Other Shapes (1986)
Grief Notes & Animal Dreams (1995)
Point No Point (2006)

point no point

poems

Jane Munro

McCLELLAND & STEWART

Library and Archives Canada Cataloguing in Publication

Munro, Jane, 1943-
Point no point / Jane Munro.

Poems.
ISBN 13: 978-0-7710-6678-8
ISBN 10: 0-7710-6678-3

I. Title.

PS8576.U574P63 2006   C811'.54   C2005-906041-7

We acknowledge the financial support of the Government of Canada through the Book Publishing Industry Development Program and that of the Government of Ontario through the Ontario Media Development Corporation's Ontario Book Initiative. We further acknowledge the support of the Canada Council for the Arts and the Ontario Arts Council for our publishing program.

Text design by Sean Tai
Typeset in Garamond by M&S, Toronto
Printed and bound in Canada

McClelland & Stewart Ltd.
75 Sherbourne Street
Toronto, Ontario
M5A 2P9
www.mcclelland.com

1 2 3 4 5   10 09 08 07 06

for
Ian Andrew Munro
Alison Elizabeth Munro
Catherine Ann Munro

The distance that the dead have gone
Does not at first appear —

Emily Dickinson, #1742

Contents

False Lily-of-the-Valley

Moving to a Colder Climate

ANOTHER STORY BUILT IN

Always, my past appears simpler than my present.

I could still walk through his family home blindfolded, push the swinging door between kitchen and dining room, and find the box of soda crackers sealed in its plastic bag in the cooler.

For the bridal tea his mother gave for me, I made a hat from a black crinoline. The cherry trees along their street were only saplings in a strip of lawn his father mowed after he'd cut the grass on the front slope. His mother raked the clippings up and dumped them in the compost behind the garage. Yellow rose bushes screened the bin from the yard where our second child, aged eleven months, walked backward and sat down on a little chair. She wore a brown sundress printed with pink flowers that I'd sewn for her.

His father died in St. Paul's Hospital seven years later. I remember the polished corridor, his blue gown, reddened eyes, and the next morning, the thunder-clap moments before the phone rang – his mother's sobs filling the line. Afterward, our son stayed with her on Tuesday nights, sleeping in sheets she'd ironed on the mangle beside the basement laundry tub. I remember her illness, her moving out, her death – and the house sold.

Now, their old home sits like a dollhouse atop a larger addition – the original front door mid-air, minus stairs. I remember the force it took to open that door, the seal in the weather-stripping you had to break.

I drive slowly round the block and up the alley, swollen with Sunday dinners I thought I'd digested. Yes, the past was good, and yes, much I've learned by heart proves transitory. Memory recomposes it under brighter lights, amidst less clutter. Yellow roses still spill over the fence. From behind, it's clear what's been added, what's changed.

CAMPING WITH MY FATHER

After the War and his broken hip and the English women he found lovely and cultivated – after the English garden of his convalescence and the khaki wool jacket with its brass buttons and his rank as captain – after he took up life with a wife and two kids and moved us to Vancouver into that first wartime house where Mother grew sweet peas and he became an insurance adjuster in his brother's company – after the earthquake when I saw the backyard roll like a wave while sitting on the kitchen counter waiting to have my hair braided – before he bought the boatyard, when I was three and my brother two, he took us camping at Boundary Bay.

His army blankets and the two canvas bedrolls smelled of preservative. He unfolded them on the sand the way mother had opened his aerogrammes. He talked of tides and pointed out the line of tangled seaweed, wood chips, and dead crabs left the night before. We slept on the beach's slant under stars.

In the morning, Mother bent by the fire cooking porridge and eggs in the boxy pans that fit inside one another. We found foggy sea glass and winkle shells, but no agates. Mother wanted a moss agate. I pestered her with milky pebbles.

He taught me to walk a log then jump to the next. Holding his hand, I squelched way, way out across the muck with its low-tide smell and warm puddles until saltchuck greeted us, cool ripples about my ankles, knees, stomach, armpits. Demonstrating the crawl, his black body hairs flattened and his mouth opened in the cave under his arm. Glancing light made me squint. Briny water in my nose tasted like pickles and wieners. He taught me to open my eyes like a fish and look up at the ocean's surprise – the silver lining of waves.

The second time he took us camping I was eleven. He taught me how to hold a pistol above my head, swing my arm down, sight along the barrel, and pull the trigger. I felt the recoil in my shoulder. The hardest part was keeping my balance. He taught me what he thought I should know, even though I was a girl.

BOATYARD

High tide at 4 a.m.
He woke me in the dark.
I rode beside him
on the chill and slippery front seat
across the old Second Narrows Bridge,
its deck thrumming under the tires,
the car's headlights
hollowing hazy tunnels
all the way to the North Shore, then
along the lower road,
down the bumpy lane,
to the tall shed on the waterfront.

On weekends, the boatyard smelled spicier
than mother's cedar chest. *She*
was also for ships. My brother and I played
under her steep hull in drifts
of fragrant sawdust.
I collected blonde ringlets –
shavings from the heavy planes
used to groom her planks –
and stuck them through my hair.

Now they'd hoisted her from the cradle
and set her at the top of the slip,
its massive tracks creosoted. The pilings below
barnacled and crusted with mussels.

He swung me onto his shoulders
and we waited. Water licked and gurgled.
Its oily gleam crept up the black timbers,
dipped like a slide into the harbour.
Seaweed smell. Tar smell. Copper paint smell.
The tweed of his jacket against my legs.
Orange tips of cigarettes.

The sky lightening as the tide came in.
Her prow on the slip above us. A few gruff words.
He stepped forward, told me, *Hold on.*
I hugged his head and pressed my ankles
against the sides of his chest.
His back twisted, and with a mighty swing, he flung
a bottle through the air. It smashed,
spilling glass and champagne
down the curve of her keel.
Cheering. Creaking. Another shout,
and the tall shadowy hull slid down the slip
and became a boat, settling in
like the other boats.
The men said, *Right pretty,*
and went about shaking hands.
I rode, buoyed by his pride,
above their heads.

Our History

in a fifties Pontiac
kissing the man I'd marry –
wet December night
the privacy
of a rain-splattered windshield –
taking off
his glasses, his pupils huge

as buffalo on a
prairie – the dark lens
of a species
we squandered – the past's long gaze
fixing us

MISSING PERSON

The last time I saw my brother he winced, pushing open the lawyer's heavy glass door into a windy downtown street. We'd just signed father's will. *Twenty'd get me to Kamloops, but forty'd be better.* No blond curls or impish grin. Hair like leaf skeletons blown across the blue eyes he got from Mother. No sparkle.

That Christmas he phoned. Making a fresh start: editing videos and glazing burl tables in Penticton. As a boy his ambidextrous pitch meant he'd be a winner. *Aim for a Rhodes Scholarship*, Father urged.

A gift for stories. Long-time cabbie. Big talker but a loner – a decade on an island, years in basement rooms, no sisters permitted. Dyslexic. Depressed. Heavy. Clever – trained as a chef – but the jobs ran out.

Lost from the bottom bunk. We used to sing each other to sleep. His bank called: loan payment and Visa overdue. Traced to Edmonton and thin air.

Flower Girl – 1949

1

When the iceman
began his progress house to house,
we scrambled onto his tailgate,
ducked into his van.
Musk rode the ice mist

into which we clambered,
fishing slivers
from wood shavings,
cramming our mouths full –
leaping off – scattering.

2

The boys two houses down rigged up a tent.
I crawled in under the old tablecloth
and they picked on me. I stuck my tongue out
and told on them. Mother made a rule:
Stay out of their yard.

The boys' grandfather sat hour after hour
on the porch of their house
under an arbour of roses,
and he called to me –
Little girl, want to see a rhinoceros?

I hung on their gate, swinging in to him,
not letting my feet touch the ground.
Where? I asked,
and he tempted me and tempted me
until I stood by his knee on one foot, holding

the toe of my other sandal behind my back.
He broke off a rose thorn
and stuck it on his nose. *There*, he said.
Then he nipped off a bigger one, licked
its hollow, and stuck it on mine.

3
After breakfast Mother braided my hair
and sent me out
until she whistled me home.
If I skinned my knee,
I could knock on the door for a Band-Aid.

She sent me for eggs
to the black house by the interurban tracks
where the mother let her children play inside,
but no sliding on the waxed linoleum.
I watched that mother whack

the head off a chicken, holding it
across the stump in her backyard,
its neck thin as kindling.
She laughed and shouted to us as the toppling
body ran round the woodpile. Dropped.

4
Unexpected visitors at breakfast.
A gardenia pumped out perfume
from the lapel of my cousin's pastel suit.
The man with her dipped his eggy knife
in Mother's jar of strawberry jam.

He'd just eaten three fried eggs.
First, he covered their eyes with salt,
then lidded them with pepper.
I stood by his elbow and stared.
He called himself a logger. Mother

said, *lumberjack*. While he wiped
his plate with toast, my cousin invited me
to be their flower girl   *yes, oh yes, please*
how my status would rise on the street
where the big girls boasted, *I've been to a wedding.*

Mother agreed to sew
the ruffled gown of white satin.
I hovered, collecting scraps of moon silk.
Stroking them against my cheek, I twirled
until dizzy, singing nonsense songs.

Father schooled me,
placing a book on my head,
drumming his fingers on the kitchen table,
singing, *See how she glides* – pacing me to lead
the bride through the cathedral.

5

When I wanted to be alone,
I climbed the rise to the vacant lot
and sank into its high weeds
flounced with spiderwebs.
There, I picked dandelions –

slitting the stems up high
and threading flower after flower
into garlands.
The big girls taught me how,
But you have to grow your fingernails.

Dandelion milk – bitter, sticky –
dripped from them
as I linked glory
to glory, descending
wreathed and crowned –

dandelion rings on my fingers,
dandelions threaded through my sandals,
dandelions tucked into my braids –
my skin smeared and reeking
with their darkening milk.

VISAGE

Like a plain plate – useful, fine in a stack, nice enough for company, just not the sort you'd display. Like a city bus – packed in rush hour, marbled with mud splashes.

> Pick a place to sit, rest your feet, but keep
> on edge. Watch for your stop.
> Calculate your exit.

Of course I'd love my face to draw in light then shimmer, but in these photographs I see uncertainty, a modified aging. It's a face to overlook: polite and compliant. I wish the two-year-old still owned my mouth. *No, no, no,* she said, wading into weeds her mother skirted, hugging a cat, lofting it on tiptoe, her black curls soft as its white belly. Cotton gloves and a plastic straw hat adjusted that face, took it to Sunday School, won it pins – a battery of them. Pins preside. While the chin's not double, its line scallops. Channels nose to lips. Eyes in gullies and a constant equivocality of expression.

> Take the veil! Go into purdah!

Fear's girl, dear contradicted face – let me be plain: I embrace you. Become the face I look out from, not others at.

Boys

Where does he go
when we linger at the table,
listening to the music –
Louis, Duke, Artie – what's
he gathering, what shedding,
as he reaches?

When his father died, his mother
and his four brothers
went to Germany for a year.
That was between the wars.
Now, all his brothers are gone –
the little boys circling his mother on the lawn.
On their birthdays he speaks of them.

And my brother – the little boy who sang
Jesus loves me this I know,
who rode in the front seat of the green Ford
and snuggled against his mother's fur jacket,
stroking its long brown hairs,
while his father
on the other side of her
bristled and snapped,
reached across and slapped him, *Quit it.*

The little boys who chased me with bracken spears
and raced by on three-speeds,

who helped build forts
and raise tadpoles, who dressed up and acted out
the parts we gave them, disappeared in cities.

Now, listening to Count Basie's
"Jumpin' at the Woodside,"
I feel him go
beyond brothers, mother, father, beyond
places he's known, past stories –
beyond the beyond of the music.

VISITATION

One morning, about five,
she burst open the door and walked in –

flung herself on the red rug –
a slender woman in a sleeveless white blouse
twisted sideways, one arm over her head.
Exhausted, she looked
heartsick, younger than I'd ever seen her,
about the age she would have been when she conceived me.

I knelt beside her, weeping
and rubbing her back, my fingers
bumping down her spine,
forehead pressing her shoulder –
the soapy smell of her skin. Oh, my
disconsolate mother,
not much older than my daughters.

Of course she'd come, I thought, she's so intuitive –
and anguished – having conceived me
as someone I've yet to become.

a high-speed car chase in San Francisco, midday, wasn't impossible then: fewer cars, fewer people – Bullitt's Mustang in the bad guys' rear-view mirror, ski jump of a hill, Alcatraz ahead, shooting past three-storey city houses, a fiery crash – but afterward, in the midst of a working harbour, Bullitt and Cathy walking into tall grass (not in any rush), afternoon sun, a breeze – I remember

how we'd tease our hair to a Brillo pad, comb a smooth layer on top, flip the ends, fix it in place – how I'd shorten a summer mini so when I bent over a desk, the skirt would just cover my ass, yes – how I'd buy forty-nine-cent pork and serve it with applesauce: an aura of Craven A and hairspray – everyone

was thin then, before pasta became popular, living on grapefruit and hard-boiled eggs and celery sticks stuffed with Velveeta – mid-week beer break in a pub: no alcohol in our efficiency apartment – magazines recycled through the laundry room, sorting the stacks: *Time, The New Yorker, Look, Life* while feeding quarters to the Bendix, discovering *The Atlantic* and *Saturday Night* – tasting bourbon for the first time one afternoon in a dim, drowsy small-town bar after driving in the pink Pontiac with its tail fins out to Lake Lemon, and every morning

cockroaches on the aquamarine cement-block wall of the kitchen – leaping out of the hide-a-bed, roll of paper towel in hand: fast and furious, we were a team, he'd flick the light on, I'd whack them (why me? the kitchen was on his side of the bed), my skin tanned golden from sunbathing even before summer started, before sunlight became a hazard, so short shorts wouldn't reveal whale-belly-white thighs, and the thing was, hats were formal: women wore hats and gloves to tea, to church, to ladies' lunches – a girdle held stockings up and going without it was like not wearing a bra, only possible in summer – walking around campus in a periwinkle blue sundress with spaghetti straps, sweat slithering down my spine

square window fan, air agitated all night, heat never letting up week after week so a sheet felt oppressive – discovering iced coffee, the air-conditioned lounge in the Student Union, sun like a piledriver as I took the shortcut home across the open field, tiger lilies in ditches

a modern time, now bathed in pearly light like a Technicolor video watched on the longest day – the first summers of adulthood: a grown-up because I was married – feeling we had to create a life for ourselves

we wrote our letters home on Friday afternoon once we'd done the cleaning – he at his desk and me at the table: an expand-o-matic opposite the hide-a-bed, you could open only one at a time – calling long distance too expensive for ordinary talk, and then Friday evening we'd go to a film in the Fine Arts building, or a drive-in movie outside of town, the speaker hooked on the open car window

we didn't know irony would sound tinny and priests lose their reputations, refrigerators poison the atmosphere and car exhausts melt slopes of permafrost in the Mackenzie Delta – we didn't guess the Selma March would fade, or that McDonald's would spawn millions the sixties seemed so full – we didn't imagine always being in a rush, or how our lives would grow more labyrinthine – it's not just the past that appears simpler than the present: the future does as well

mid-life – lots of footage running through my mind that I rarely think to look at

The Ear of the Heart

FLAX

such a sunlit sky
   the blue of wild flax
sky's pool
   flower after flower
   gone as mornings go
so much blue behind me

A long freight train drawn
across the prairie like a tape marked
Pull Here – green cattle cars, brown flat cars,
silver tankers: a sentence moving its burden elsewhere.
Word after word used over and over. Transports
tying a country together.
The slow strip of a whistle uncovers
longing the way spreading a lather of suds down
my arms in the shower and watching a spray undress me
to the skin again arouses an echo of earlier days
when buttons
were for undoing. The way I longed to
speak French after a trip to Percé. Riding a little train
across the Gaspé, seeing into the backyards of villages.
A woman hanging out her wash waving
to me, and a man
in a pickup stopping behind a dropped
crossing gate, getting out of his cab, and nodding at cars
rolling by, their wheels squealing.
I began to build another
vocabulary,
laying crossties week after week, imagining
a new country opening up, but I never laid enough
rail to ride. Now the wish for another language
relinquished, or so I thought,
but the freight

rumbling east pulls my eyes along its line
the way, from time to time, I'm astonished by my life –
its many branch lines – its
impossibility.

Listen with the Ear of the Heart

away from home
I hear him
turn over in his sleep

but it's just the leaves –
my window open
halfway up a tree

faint thunder
and a light downpour
like an exhalation

he talks in his sleep –
I am used to hearing
without deciphering

how can I miss him
in the middle of an elm
simmering with small birds?

Half a Continent Away

a scratching
outside his window
toenails on a wooden beam –

the little raccoon
who climbs like a squirrel
drops onto the tray of seed
and starts to eat,
messy as the jays who toss
showers of millet, pick out
black sunflower seeds –

their oiled hulls
upturned boats
on an ochre beach

Django Blues

Gypsy at the river, fishing – broke fingers grab a trout.
Gypsy at the river, fishing – broke fingers grab a trout.
Can't find him 'cause he's playing on his own –
can't find him 'cause he's playing on his own.
He's catching time – eating them fine bones.

Tambourine girl whirling – feet fish flirting with the ripple of a creek.
Tambourine girl whirling – feet fish flirting with the ripple of a creek.
Can't see her 'cause she's circling on her own –
can't see her 'cause she's circling on her own.
She's catching time – shaking them fine bones.

Django played a delta's temper – salt and sweet, his river swinging.
Django played a delta's temper – salt and sweet, his river swinging.
Can't call him 'cause he's listening on his own –
can't call him 'cause he's listening on his own.
He's catching time – surprising them fine bones.

TULIPS

Four vases lipping tulips, lapping tipped petals – yellow orange green red tulips – waffled petals motley, ruffled, cupped petals atop crystal vases, rag green leaves loose and untied like baggy pants unstrung. Under the vases books and papers, and downstairs a bed pulled out for me.

She's had house guests all week and men from both sides of the coin: Mr. Mind and Mr. Body – heads or tails – it's a toss-up. Tulips kiss with lips pursed, a form mercurial, erect then floppy. I'd take the one who makes spirit rise –

ah, the green stem –

tulips in a school-room drawing. Tulips for tables and counters. Slosh of dishwasher beside the stove and *The Journal of Consciousness Studies*. I've spread *The New York Times* under tulips to read Tuesday's science section about the binding problem and recent theory re: the rhythm of integration. It says we're flash and furor, firing neurons, escaping steam, but these tulips – I think four vases full – I think women with sumptuous histories, and how cells in their littleness lift

tulip heads like little operas,
like Cleopatra, like Bessie Smith,
like my sister or this
poet-friend

The Wind Is Resting

sitting a while
just breathing in the grasses

having wrestled with this place
all night, as if trapped
in the spruce trees and poplar bush
rolling back and forth
on the mat of harrowed field
gathering momentum to push harder –
as if the task of turning us over into morning

fell on its shoulders:
the wind needn't strain so –
it's distressing to hear it
obsessed and fretting
unable to stop.

He leaned forward to open his eightieth birthday presents,
and we could read what was written on his back:
BlackAdder, the name on the T-shirt
showing through the dress shirt.
And under his skin –
the writing on his lungs, the black crabs
in the wave caves of his chest
where the inspirations
and the exhalations
came and went. He a beachhead
where tides sounded. Because they beat against him
we heard the voices of an unvoiced ocean,
but it wasn't water
we heard in his words – no, it was land: stone
and thin soil and horses.
We heard geology and our history. We heard men.
When I say that now, in the little cave of the word,
his presence, there with crabs, *BlackAdder* – viper
and comic – and horses, but also a roofer
hung from a spire without a ladder,
and a husband forcing the land open with his thumbs,
breaking it to feed himself and his family.

GREAT HORNED OWL

Looking for the owl
a bit early – the sky still lucid blue
with a few downy cirrus.
As usual, hoping
for magic – a textbook
silhouette on a tree branch
at the edge of the field: *whoooo*
would you be, walking my way?
its ears perked up,
grooming from its nimbus
a key to unlock these days
of not expecting much, having greyed
like the driest summer on record
to colours in the owl's range.
Not that it would speak to me –
I'd just overhear it
like the radio. Driving into town, a voice
reading a story's first line, *Some things don't change.*
Oh yeah? Like what, I say, feeling pissed-off
by mutability, glaciers retreating up peaks,
smog a yellowing bruise above the city –
why so irritated these days? Get out of the car,
on with the errands. God, it's as if there's
no refuge – nothing lined
with breast feathers. You watch a man age
the way wood weathers: cracks deepening,
surface slivering – each brush with death

polishing memories. As a child,
it was one of the spooky questions – where's space?
When you're outside of everyplace,
is there an address? The owl wasn't there.
Hearing wind's traffic in silence
along a tractor trail
between ploughed field and poplar bush.
Noticing the first pale tuft tangled in grass,
bending for it. So, I was, after all, in the right place –
fluff from a fledgling owl,
then larger vanes rippled in umber and pearl.
Collecting a bouquet of feathers –
a marvel sufficient to the night.

Frog

Sheets of lightning stretched
from west to east like a line of laundry
snapping in the wind.

A tempest to the south, but overhead
the Big Dipper slowly stirs the constellations,
keeping them from sticking.

Who can sleep? I'm blown tree to tree,
silk pyjamas flapping from my knees,
a frog's skin across my breast.

I remember twenty years ago sliding out of bed
to walk naked through starlight
across a granite bluff, my bare feet

picking up the rock's stored heat,
squatting to pee and staring
at the egg-masses of galaxies in their milky gel.

No end to promise then. Now mid-life
this midnight: high pressure, low pressure –
I've lost the courage for wishing.

How to befriend
this changeling: my plain
and slippery, new-old self?

A friend screamed each time I said, *I'm sorry.*
A friend sent me a gold cup.
A friend washed her father's bones.

I need to put my finger on
a frog hidden in my heart –
feel it, struggling, in my palm.

CROWS

Exhumed from night's midden of thunder, I come
into daylight feeling garish.

The crows this morning yell
like angry old men. Who am I hearing
as their voices shout down my dream –
the one where I cry *help*
but can't make a peep.

Clouds trail virga of rain.
The crows strut on the melting chocolate
of a newly wetted field.
Behind them canola – a dimpled lemon layer
on lime Jello-O – bright as penny candy.

Mud cakes the soles of my sneakers.
We're left to guess what passes
from one creature into another.
If I cracked my dream,
what might hatch in my throat?

Apparition

On the eleventh day of running, coming up to the bend, I saw two
figures – ghostly in colour, subtle in nature – in the air above the gravel.

The taller was myself; the smaller was a man-fetus, attached to my ankle
by his umbilicus. He dragged me down though we both floated. His
knees drawn up, his body hunched, he couldn't walk. I, off-kilter and
tilted, tugged him along, keeping us moving with my strong legs. We'd
travelled a long way through an aura of dust.

Shocked to see him, appalled at my situation – shackled to a goblin,
not the brother born but another who'd slipped out of his un-birth on
my heels. Such grotesquery. What to do? He must hate me dragging
him through all my tasks and relationships. And me, hobbled. Oh,
come midwife

with your scissors.
Come undertaker. Come gravedigger.
Come stone carver. Come priest.
Come blessing.
Shrive him. Shroud him in a cabbage leaf.
Magpies, drop feathers for his mattress.
Unfurl the cramped limbs, the humped spine.
Stroke clenched feet and fingers open.
Cover him with sweet peas and mound prairie soil above.
Plant sage and chamomile.
Pray he sleeps long and well.

Give me the weeds for grieving and set me free.

False Lily-of-the-Valley

POINT NO POINT

It's a ten-minute walk – down the gravel drive with its mossy centre strip, across the highway, into a maze of trails winding through tall salal and wind-stunted alder to the beach. This is my headland. On a map, it's a promontory that's a point from one side, not the other: Point No Point. On foot, a network of trails tunnelling the bush. One path opens to a pebbled bay, another burrows up a creek bed. A spur to the edge of a bluff carves a window, framing a view of white-capped waves and further points along the shoreline.

We left the city, moving to this coast and its colder climate when I turned fifty and wanted to change my life. What was I expecting?

February: salmonberries spurt new leaves, lady ferns climb the trunks of trees, catkins dangle from twigs, and Methuselah's beard drifts from branches. Inside the matted second growth the sound of the wind is muted.

Out on the point, cormorants and gulls queue in the gale and stare across the strait at the Olympics. A trawler gurgles by. I think of the smell of coffee and diesel as I step carefully on wet rock, the swell and dip of the deck. A cormorant stretches its neck, rises to tiptoe, lifts – its wings spread like hands pushing down on the give of air.

They say in Kashmir each carpet has a song. An elder sits at the head of the bench and sings its changes – notes the rug's colours and knots – and that's how they know what to weave.

Above the bluff a raven plummets in turbulence, sweeps up, then glides out of sight on a cross-current. The same salt air laden with spray buffeting me on this prow is flexing spruce and Nootka roses, shaping the landscape.

Wind's labyrinth. What do I expect?

SALMONBERRIES

Later, things will get brutish.
I will squat, tug,
swing the mattock, work my fingers
round their knobby taproots,
fall over backward, all
to get the goddamned salmonberries
out of the meadow. But today
I pause to see their delicate green dressing
of April's raw flank – as if a blade had scraped
the scales off winter, then wrapped its ache
in seaweed. Salmonberry leaves
spring from sinewy branches. Each leaf
points toward the sky. Each flower,
a magenta bell, hangs down. A winter wren,
tail tipped up, extends and extends its song.
I turn back to the house thinking
leaves, flowers, bird –
wrapped in neat bundles like sushi.

Morning with Cats

I wake to fog, white and silent, flowing over the roof,
swirling into the clearing, muffling even the varied thrushes
who yesterday called like phones ringing from the woods.

The cats in their thick coats, me in a flannel nightie,
padding down to the kitchen. Chill air harsh in my nostrils.
Light the stove – a murmur of flames, their blue leaves

rustling under the steel grill. I should light the furnace
but all that work would break the spell –
scraping creosote, snapping kindling, splitting wood – no,

not today. Instead, I put on Mahler's Fourth.
A child's view of heaven: sleigh bells, angels baking bread,
good asparagus, good apples, good pears. The cats

go in and out. I sit close to the back door
so I can open it without getting up. A little wind stirs the fog,
lifting thimbleberry leaves – their pale undersides flutter.

It's an ocean fog, harvesting droplets far from shore
then unrolling them across new sorrel and the daffodils
bordering the woodshed like a kindergarten frieze.

Lieder from a hundred years ago – calling a child
who'd wake early in a house stilled by slumber to read,
curled under her quilt, the book closed at lights out.

Fog coats the windows with seed pearls. Music loves
the kitchen's plain details. I watch one cat drink rapidly.
We eat a little. What a lush romance to have a life.

Monk

he plays
the piano
like it's an animal
he's figuring
to touch
its haunch, its tail something
it still chases
not straight, no chart, plays
like he's got a hunch
there's something
he will do
it likes

ELLA: AN ELEGY

Swing it Ella, Louis hands it to you
early fifties
a recording studio
you got good legs, open-toed sandals
a kid could ride your cushiony hip
while you serve the music
steaming Berlin songs
"Cheek to Cheek," "Isn't This a Lovely Day?"
and basins of Gershwin
Louis's growl
his horn-rimmed glasses and wide grin
white ankle socks rolled over, black loafers
trumpet and hankic on his lap
the two of you sit on folding chairs
as if at a church supper
where there's food enough for all

False Lily-of-the-Valley

Invisibly, *Maianthemum dilatatum* laces
the borders of a trail with its
ghostly rhizomes, then
lances the debris of dilapidated leaves, raising
furled green umbrellas, opening
into hearts afloat on stems.
Come May, racemes arise
stippling trail's edge
and forest floor. They gel
into mottled berries
that ripen red and nod, luminous
under autumn rains.
Maianthemum – in the small of the bluff's back –
false to no one, true to itself.

suited up
as if this coastal jungle were an English common
as if they were on their way to a party, her hat
decked with roses or maybe they're peonies
such a neat waist for a mother of six, such
a sweet face, the grandmother
who died before I could meet her
for whom I'm named
the Jane he called Jenny
my childhood friend my grandfather
the one who taught me to paint
ultramarine for the mountains, Prussian blue for the sea
only he's dapper much younger
the same pipe in his teeth but also a fedora
the one who told me he called her name
over and over again after she died
until she came to him
as if she'd just stepped in from the garden
he showed me how he'd stood then
beside his easel by an open door
and how close she was as she comforted him
in the photograph their hats are part
of a grammar of ornament
what to wear when walking through woods
it could have been Point No Point
where these English lovers
strolled on a Sunday through towering sword ferns

named something they didn't know
in the Pacheedaht tongue
each frond studded
with Braille dots letting go smaller dots
brown on his fingers
caught in the lace of her blouse

FISHBOAT BAY

On the eve of the last sockeye opening
twenty perhaps thirty seiners
rafted together
in the lee of Point No Point, waiting
for a tide silver with salmon
tasting their way home.
Before dawn they'd gone, but that night
the buzz between boats was effervescent.

They haven't come again
though the bay's now named for them.
Will they ever return? The way my father
traced his steps back
to the front hall of a long-ago home
by recalling the chill of a marble table under his thighs
as his sister laced his boots
and also the taste
of a tomato sandwich on fresh brown bread.

SPINDRIFT

Westerly streaming over the roof
loud as river rapids,
house creaking like a
schooner under sail, ghosts,
gulls, a lantern on the yardarm,
electricity out twelve hours, wind and rain

the same for centuries
scouring cove and cave, old hemlock
uprooted at the edge of the meadow,
cormorants pumping hard
hang stationary in the lee of the point,
seafoam thick and dirty

sheared from ocean, flung
hip-deep across rocks and logs,
storm carding whitecaps, flinging spume
curls to the top of a cliff, tatters
caught in spruce, tufts of foam on trails,
white tags on cabin windows –

I grab a tree trunk
then let the dense current
carry me on its spiral up the path, its push
a cushion, rough magic, at my back.

WINTER SOLSTICE

Ovid says the gods
still the battery of storms
to allow the Halcyon's newest chick
the days it needs to fledge.

I wish.

Ovid's kingfishers
gather twigs and moss, skim
whitecaps, select a wave, weave a nest.
Could this feeble sun be their hatchling?

Flushed into the coming year,
it drifts, horizon to horizon.
How will it widen the days?
Hard to feel that pendulum
gain momentum.

Addressing Predators

On the radio, the gentleness
in the woman's voice demonstrates
how she talks to grizzlies. *Take out all modulation*
in pitch, and praise the bear's beauty.
She lives without a gun on the tip of Kamchatka
amongst seven hundred grizzlies.
Her attitude is her armour.
When you meet a bear, she says,
drop to the ground, look around,
relax into the landscape.
                              Once a black bear waded
through shoulder-high salal, came to stare
at the kitchen's glass door, us at table.
He strolled between raised beds, swung his head
at the compost, and entered the meadow.
In the sun his fur looked buttered, even creamy.
Oh, beautiful bear, such a fine fellow . . . but hearing my voice,
he charged up the berm, haunches churning,
and disappeared in salmonberries.

                    Our island of forest absorbed him,
but it's shrinking. Fir, hemlock, spruce, cedar, harvested by whining
machinery. Lumbering Caterpillars with long arms grab a trunk, slice
its butt, strip branches and bark, then drop the log on a stack. Howling.
Growling. Blue tapes knotted on mashed salal where, under the slash,

water trickles. The odd culvert shored with gravel. When they're gone what's left is muted, but not gentled.

A week ago, leaving a silent clear-cut, I entered the next cut block, as yet unsurveyed. Cougar prints. Fresh. A patch of mud. Creek roar nearby. Second growth timber plenty big enough for a ninety-pound cat to lie on a limb. Sleeper gone to ground in a receding forest, camouflaged. At the mouth of this creek, one ate a raccoon on our neighbour's deck. Cougars hunt humans. I'd like to see his vertical pupils, muscled body, but – *Don't even think of it, Lion!* I shout, swing a stick, hightail it for the open.

Down below, Chew Excavating's started making gravel. Clatter of shattering stone, whoosh as a load fills a dump truck. We're so far from Kamchatka.

—✦—

When you talk to a dump truck, use every
tone in your voice. Make it shriek
and whisper and growl. Be a mother
grizzly with cubs, territorial.

Sometime, when quiet returns, I will
listen for song. Praise as fog praises.
Settle into the weave of forest, shore – relax
into the landscape.

DURATION

in the dark
before another day
feeling my way down the hall

surf below the house
a hum
from the refrigerator

hand following the bookcase
bare toes
tapping for the edge of a step

that the heart
never fails to complete its journey
like the sun

VOICE MAIL

Full moon – I step out into the yard – it's climbed the laddered branches of the driveway fir and travels in the open, cratered and bright. Noise of water like traffic – creek down there, kick-heeled, scrambling through its chasm – and below us, combers blooming white before collapsing on the beach. Where I'm standing a spruce tree grew, too knotted to make studs or decking. Part of it burning now in the fireplace – smoke – its soft smudge in the moonlight.

When we moved in, our old grey cat wandered in the woods for three weeks. We'd glimpse a shape between trees – I searched through the rain, calling, stopping, listening. That same weekend my father died and I would never hear his voice again. I have his answering machine with the tape I can't bear to play   he'd understand   he always said, *A question's more important than the answer.*

Messages invisible in phone lines, words from down under, back east. What traces are worth keeping?

I go inside.

In the morning, long after the moon has vanished, we find ice crystals have crept from crevices in the soil.

Moving to a Colder Climate

MOVING TO A COLDER CLIMATE

Out here, we discovered
fog is an element. Flowing down
the grooved metal roof, curling up
as it hits gravel, leaping into spruce,
shrouding cedar. We breathe it
when just a little inland
sunshine shreds it. I've learned
to run my fingers under hot water, layer
sweaters. Below us, the creek's mouth
inhales the clouds ocean exhales.
Needles drip. We stack wood,
split kindling, keep a space heater by the bed.
What did I expect?

Not my father's death –
as if he'd chosen
the timing – signing
our move with his – articulating
its history.
We had milled timber
from the trees cut when clearing.
Twelve-inch beams, full-dimension studs.
It was never easy
to please him, but in building this house
I came close.
He studied our plans,
followed each stage of construction,

even came out here once
just after the forms were poured
when the earth was raw and muddy,
the crew dripping in their slickers –
thumped across the plywood under-floor with his cane,
checked the start of framing,
then demanded
we drive back into town
for Scotch. Wine was not a manly spirit.

And spirits helped him to his end.
After the Remembrance Day service,
while we were packing boxes,
after drinks at the Yacht Club,
he took a taxi home mid-afternoon –
grey light, flecks of snow.
Eighty-five, almost eighty-six,
sixty per cent disabled,
he fell on the concrete steps
outside his apartment.
The taxi driver called an ambulance.
It wasn't serious – only ribs broken –
but he got pneumonia in hospital.

How could he succumb
to such a run-of-the-mill disease
after two broken hips,
the fusion of four vertebrae,
a smashed shoulder, wrecked elbow, dropped foot,
two hip replacements,

gall bladder surgery, one
yard of intestine gone, deep burns
to his scalp from the house fire?

The nurses moved him closer to their station
three times: he would not stay in bed.

He died six years to the hour
after the inferno filled the log house
as if it were a stove,
its thick walls holding in – intensifying – the fire.
He'd built the house for Mother,
the house he said killed her –
his carpentry, his design – and after that
he wouldn't build a thing.
She got out and he shouted at her
Now, for God's sake, stay out!
but she headed in again to get a hose.

With her, he'd placidly listen to family chatter.
Alone, he'd miss its flow, lose its swing, his gaze
sad and steady through those
scratched glasses –
the glasses I once took to the Ladies' to wash
and polished on my skirt.
On my last visit, I left him
seated at a small table with his bottle of Scotch, waiting
for a friend. At the door, I turned to wave, to blow a kiss,
and he just nodded – no smile. Pain

was his body's armature.
All his organs and systems are breaking down,
the doctor said, taking away his driver's licence –
afterward asking
if he'd been depressed, saying,
We could have treated that.

Gripping a flashlight
the winter after the fire, I entered
the burned-out house –
its tumult of sagging beams, dropped rafters,
gutted rooms –
bending to probe cinders, trembling.
Out of that sludge he
created blame –
named it his fault
to build the log house for her, not realizing
it could turn into a furnace. So:

a charred house and a new house.

Why didn't I expect his death?
Our move, his move,
checkmate.
His advice: *Watch for patterns.*
Think ahead. He taught me
to pin drafting paper
on a drawing board, slide
a T-ruler, connect points, project
a line. Once, he showed me

how to conduct a survey
with sexton, rod, and chain
the way he'd measured a valley
starting from a lookout tower.
Now, I wish
I'd turned around, rushed
back to the city to sit with him,
hold his hand.
But it was like him
to go alone, as the spirit moved him.
He used to say, *Always be ready
to hop in the car and take off.*
What held me up?

Moving to Point No Point
was coming home to
a hand-built house,
to woods redolent of childhood.

                      Is death

also a surveyor's term, a point
when viewed from life, but no point,
seen from the other side?

At the drafting table I see those hands,
large versions of my own –
even now when I spread my fingers
I'm measuring them
digit to digit, palm to palm
against his – leaf of the same pattern.

*I'd rather have an idea
than a child,* he said. When he disappeared

into his thoughts I knew
he'd gone prospecting once again,
splitting rock on the wall of a canyon,
following a river, dodging
grizzlies and cougars – *Daddy,
tell us about prospecting.* He could

disappear right in front of us,
shed his attention,
change season, withdraw, and then

reappear.
That spring of his coming back!

When the war was over
he came back and moved us all –
suddenly, we belonged to him –
from Chilliwack to Vancouver. All except
Smudge-Cat – *No cats in my house* –
loaded into the Austin,
driven past cabbage fields and pastures,
down to the city. *You can
have a dog,* he said. So I chose
a yapping wire-haired terrier – Mike –
who would chase the paperboy, catch kittens
and chickens, and kill them. *Daddy?* I could

ask him anything, *have you ever*
seen a vision? So he told me
about the lady in the blue cloud. How
he'd scaled Goat, bushwhacked
across a valley back of Dam,
and gotten lost. Sixteen,
alone on a precipice. The lady
in the blue cloud hovered over him
while he lay on the rock ledge and stared at her, crying
he was so filled up with joy. Next day
he followed tributaries
until he found the river out, hacking
through Devil's Club twelve feet high, its spiky stems
thick as a hammer's haft, and got home
in time for Sunday dinner. His mother, at the sink,
told him to wash up and change his clothes.

He'd tell this tale with pride: his mother knew
she needn't worry. But I saw a sweaty kid
at the kitchen door, brambles in his sleeves, and

the lady above him in her blue cloud –
the blue of forget-me-nots, of Mother's eyes.
Tell me more about the blue lady –
but he'd have moved on to survival,
bushcraft. *Don't get stuck,* he'd say,
like I did. Pick your way down
while you're going up. And when you're lost, remember,
follow water.

At seven,
once he could swim the Gorge,
his father gave him a canoe and a rifle.
At fourteen,
after scaling Mount Crown on his own,
he straddled the rim of its crater
and watched a party, roped together, climb toward him.
At forty-four,
his boatyard went broke, his partner
disappeared. To pay off the debt,
Mother went back to teaching, and by then
he'd started building the log house. We moved in with
his table saw in the middle of the room,
sawdust carried out before we ate our supper.

For four years
we lived in the first section:
twenty-five-feet square. Their bed a davenport,
my sister's crib by the back door behind a sheet,
my brother and I sharing a tiny bunkroom.
That first winter, only the fireplace for heat.
I remember its golden light flickering
on the rounds of newly barked logs
and the mice
darting across the flagstone hearth.

Things were happiest when he worked
on the huge grain elevators –
at times watching concrete pour all night
into towering silos.

There were blueprints
and pencil drafts. I leafed through sheets
of his plans for dust control.
At Alberta Wheat Pool
I collected pill bottles filled with grains
that sat on my bookshelves for years –
durum, soft red, Marquis, rape, rye, barley.
In those days he'd bring an encyclopedia
to the dinner table, or an atlas
with rail lines cross-hatched and their passes labelled,
for an explanation of the Crow Rate.

Once, when I was with Ranjan, my Bengali lover,
we dropped in – or, tried to –
for a visit. Father
wouldn't let us through the door.
Months later,
after I'd held his grandchildren hostage –
None of us will enter your house
until you welcome Ranjan –
they invited us to tea.
Father was polite, having
worked up India in the *Encyclopedia Britannica*.
When my sister fell for a Frenchman,
he'd declared, *No*
daughter of mine will embrace
a foreign tongue.

Nor would we fall
for juvenile pulp fiction – Nancy Drew, detective, or

Cherry Ames, nurse. Checking the stack
I'd brought home from school, he ordered,
Take them back. Tell the librarian
your father forbids you to read such trash. I told her,
His rule is I must read two non-fiction books
for every book of fiction. She gestured
to the shelves in that cement-blocked
cell and asked, *From here?*

Habitually, Mother covered
his serving of supper with a lid
and set it on the heater in the family room.
He'd come in late, eat,
scrape the plate,
and sit alone, smoking.

When guests were coming,
he'd rant about our mess – a hairbrush on the counter,
shoes under a chair, papers on the hearth.
He'd grab a carton and patrol the house.
What's this doing here? he'd shout, tossing things in.
Later, we'd dig through the teetering boxes
beside the furnace, recovering belongings.
If we were missing a sock or a library book,
Mother would ask, *Have you looked in the storage room?*

Sometimes I'd rub his back
as he lay on the bed, hurting too much
to stand up.
This man can do anything,

an Army psychologist had written.
*You are very lucky to have
such a gifted father,*
                said my mother.

Our fights unpredictable –
blow-ups out of nothing – he'd rage at me
and I'd snap back, infuriated
by unfairness – *The law says you must obey me
until you turn twenty-one.*
Mother shouting, *Stop it! You must not do this!*
Once I locked myself in the bathroom,
took my quilt, meant to stay – though I remember
eyeing the window and wondering
about secretly climbing out.

He'd urge, *To thine own self be true,*
then swear, *I will make a woman of you,*
by which he meant
pleasant, conventional, deferential,

decorative. Women found him attractive.
Men, he told me,
*like to make a splash
so they toss pebbles in a pond.
Smart women
ripple just a little,
then a little more again –
keep a man interested.* I held

a board while he hammered,
fetched a book when he wanted to look something up.
Give me a hand, will you? he'd ask,
turning to find me.
In those years he wanted
a Viking burial – lashed to a burning boat, sent out to sea.

Six months after his death
he came back again.
I was in the living room
of the house that burned down –
New Year's Eve – a knock
on the front door, and
there he was, triumphant, grinning,
holding out a bottle of Scotch and a loaf of bread,
first-footing us
as his younger self – a man of forty – Daddy
come home.

Later on, I was running
while thinking about him, about his lady
in a blue cloud – and found
a Swiss Army knife
on the side of the road.
I carry it with me.
And his advice:
You have all the tools you need.
Now, for God's sake, use them!
Also carried with me, him

pounding the patio table with his shoe, *No*
daughter of mine will put herself
before her children.

But he spent weeks when my marriage ended
ripping out a wall in the front hall,
freeing archways,
opening up the old house we'd moved into
to better suit his stubborn damn fool of a daughter
who never could explain to him
what on God's green earth
justified her actions. *It's not that I doubt your intelligence,*
he'd say, *but you lack experience.*

I have lost many dear ones, he explained,
lying in my son's bed after the fire –
homeless, wifeless – not wanting sympathy.

But six years later,
in tears at the kitchen table, how
he missed her – *all the time – every day – sometimes*
every hour – she took such pleasure in life –
the truth is, I'd go with her anywhere
just to watch her delight. Now, I see him

standing on the plywood under-floor as he
toasted our home-to-be.
I imagine him sitting in this finished kitchen,
as he never did, arguing about

drying firewood, or when to call a woman a lady,
as the fog rolls in again. Strands
blow across the house, then
deepen to that bone-marrow chill.
Dripping from spruce needles, raining
only under trees. Cloud
hiding all depth in vision and in sound.
Then, breaking up – sun
lighting a bank of cumulus over the strait,
and between the treetops, scraps of blue –
wind vane swinging, wind chimes ringing.

Don't get stuck – pick
your way down while you're going up – and
there he is,
in gumboots and slicker,
headed for the creek, and – *when*
you're lost,
               follow water.

Acknowledgements

Earlier versions of poems in this collection have appeared in the following magazines: *The Antigonish Review, Canadian Author, Canadian Literature, The Fiddlehead, The Malahat Review,* and *The Massachusetts Review.* "Django Blues" was published in *Why I Sing the Blues,* edited by Jan Zwicky and Brad Cran (Smoking Lung Press, 2001). "Crows," "Frog," and "Great Horned Owl" were published in *Listening with the Ear of the Heart* (St. Peter's Press, 2003), edited by Dave Margoshes and Shelley Sopher. "Intercourse" was anthologized in *Following the Plough: Recovering the Rural,* edited by John B. Lee (Black Moss Press, 2000). "Boatyard" was anthologized in the League of Canadian Poets's *Vintage 97–98* (Quarry Press, 1998). "Intercourse" received honourable mention in the 1997 George Woodcock Poetry Contest; "Boatyard" received honourable mention in the 1998 National Poetry Contest.

Many thanks to Don McKay for his careful reading and helpful suggestions; to Roo Borson, Jan Conn, Lorna Crozier, Becky Helfer, Mary di Michele, Ian Munro, and Jan Zwicky for their encouragement and thoughtful advice; and to Bob Amussen for his fine editorial eye and faith in my writing.

I am grateful to the Saskatchewan Writers Guild's Writers/Artists Colonies for providing me, summer after summer, with space and time to work on poetry, and to the Canada Council for the Arts for financial support while I was finishing this collection.